STEM IS EVERYWHERE

T0118883

JOHN LESLEY

EARTH IS MY HOME

EARTH SCIENCES

REDBACK publishing

Redback Publishing
PO Box 357 Frenchs Forest NSW 2086
Australia

www.redbackpublishing.com
orders@redbackpublishing.com

© Redback Publishing 2022

ISBN 978-1-922322-84-5

All rights reserved. No part of this publication may be reproduced in any
form or by any means (including photocopying or storing it in any medium
by electronic means and whether or not transiently or incidentally to
some other use of this publication) without the written permission of
the copyright owner. Applications for the copyright owner's written
permission should be addressed to the publisher.

Author: John Lesley
Editor: Marlene Vaughan
Designer: Redback Publishing

Original illustrations © Redback Publishing 2022
Originated by Redback Publishing

Printed and bound in Malaysia

Acknowledgements
Abbreviations: l—left, r—right, b—bottom, t—top, c—centre, m—middle
We would like to thank the following for permission to reproduce
photographs: (Images © shutterstock) p12tm https://www.nasa.gov/sites/
default/files/thumbnails/image/don_pettit_on_iss.jpg. p21b by Aerial-i,

Every effort has been made to contact copyright holders of any material
reproduced in this book. Any omissions will be rectified in subsequent
printings if notice is given to the publisher.

Disclaimer
All the internet addresses (URLs) given in this book were valid at the time
of going to press. However, due to the dynamic nature of the internet,
some addresses may have changed, or sites may have changed or ceased
to exist since publication. While the author and publisher regret any
inconvenience this may cause readers, no responsibility for any such
changes can be accepted by either the author or the publisher.

A catalogue record for this
book is available from the
National Library of Australia

CONTENTS

OUR OWN CORNER OF THE UNIVERSE

PLANET EARTH

EARTH IS THE ONLY PLACE IN THE UNIVERSE WHERE WE KNOW FOR CERTAIN THAT LIFE EXISTS

Earth is the third planet from the Sun

A rocky planet with a core of iron

Has one natural satellite, the Moon

4.5 billion years old

The 'Goldilocks Planet'- not too hot and not too cold - just right for life

In constant motion

FOR HUMANS AND ALL OTHER LIFE ON THIS PLANET, EARTH IS THE MOST PRECIOUS PLACE IN THE UNIVERSE

WHY ALL THE FUSS ABOUT WATER?

We only have to turn on a tap or walk down to the beach and we have access to lots of water. Why is there such a fuss about conserving it?

Without fresh water, life as we know it cannot exist. Living things in the salty water of the oceans still need to carry around their own water inside their bodies, both in their blood and inside their cells. Plants and animals that live on land also carry their own water with them inside their bodies.

ABOUT 60% OF OUR BODY IS MADE UP OF WATER

When Earth first formed from a cloud of gases and dust, billions of years ago, there were no oceans, lakes or rivers of water. These did not form until Earth was about 3.8 billion years old. Before that, the Earth was too hot, and water turned into steam.

WHERE DID OUR WATER COME FROM?

The hydrogen and oxygen that make up water came from the huge mass of matter that eventually formed our Solar System. Earth's water was later increased when comets and asteroids fell onto the surface, bringing their water with them.

WANDERING CONTINENTS

We all know that animals migrate across the globe. Believe it or not, the continents are also moving!

The land masses we call continents have not always been where they are now. In a process called plate tectonics, the land on the surface of the Earth is slowly moving. Australia has drifted 1.5 metres northwards in the last twenty five years. India used to be an island until 50 million years ago, when it collided with Asia, creating the Himalayan mountains.

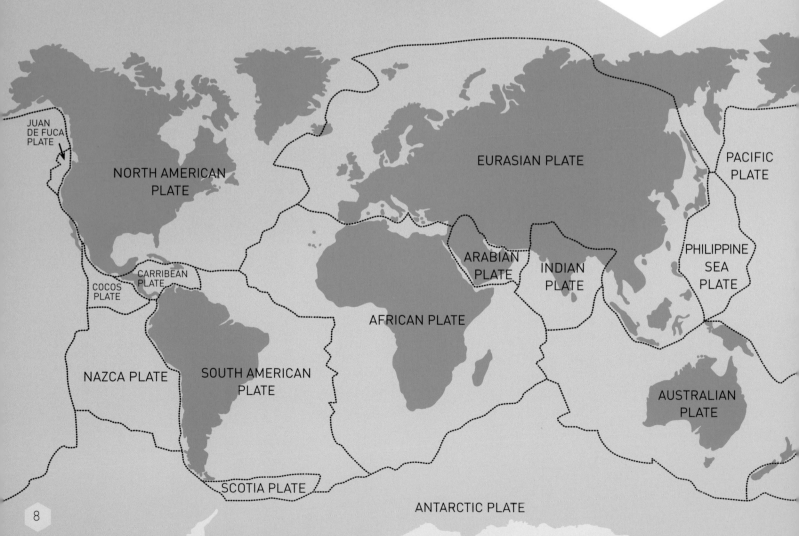

JUAN DE FUCA PLATE

NORTH AMERICAN PLATE

EURASIAN PLATE

PACIFIC PLATE

COCOS PLATE

CARRIBEAN PLATE

ARABIAN PLATE

INDIAN PLATE

PHILIPPINE SEA PLATE

AFRICAN PLATE

NAZCA PLATE

SOUTH AMERICAN PLATE

AUSTRALIAN PLATE

SCOTIA PLATE

ANTARCTIC PLATE

PANGEA AND GONDWANA

Two of the Earth's ancient continents are called Pangea and Gondwana. As they split apart and moved around the globe, they formed the continental land masses of today.

PANGAEA   LAURASIA AND GONDWANA   PRESENT

200 MILLION YEARS AGO   120 MILLION YEARS AGO

FOSSILS

The breaking up of the ancient continents has left similar fossils in modern countries that are now separated by large oceans.

Fossils of Glossopteris, a tree that thrived 300 million years ago, are found in Australia, India, South Africa, South America and Antarctica. Although they are now oceans apart, all of these land masses were once joined together, allowing plants and animals to spread easily from one area to another.

THE AIR AROUND US

Life only exists in a very thin region over the surface of the Earth. Seen from space, the layer of air that keeps us all alive looks very thin and fragile.

OZONE LAYER

Ozone is a special form of oxygen in the atmosphere. The ozone layer can block ultraviolet rays from the Sun. When we pollute the atmosphere with damaging gases, the ozone can be destroyed, resulting in higher ultraviolet levels at the surface of the Earth.

UV LIGHT

ATMOSPHERE

UV LIGHT

Ultraviolet light is one of the causes of skin cancer.

WHAT THE ATMOSPHERE DOES FOR US

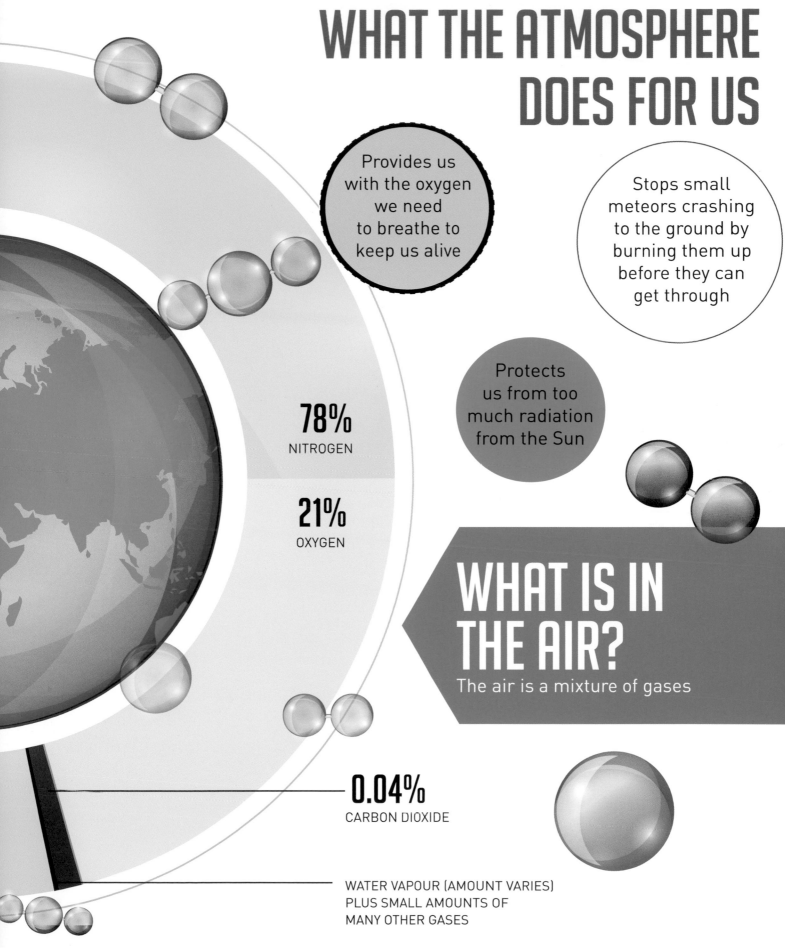

Provides us with the oxygen we need to breathe to keep us alive

Stops small meteors crashing to the ground by burning them up before they can get through

Protects us from too much radiation from the Sun

78%
NITROGEN

21%
OXYGEN

WHAT IS IN THE AIR?
The air is a mixture of gases

0.04%
CARBON DIOXIDE

WATER VAPOUR (AMOUNT VARIES)
PLUS SMALL AMOUNTS OF
MANY OTHER GASES

EARTH IN THE SOLAR SYSTEM

Our Earth is like a spaceship in space. It is constantly moving and it provides us with everything we need to live.

We are on the third planet from the Sun and our Solar System is just one of billions in the Milky Way Galaxy.

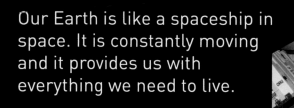

RUBBISH

In a spaceship, astronauts keep rubbish and waste stored on board. They cannot just dump it into space. The Earth is like a giant spaceship. When we throw something away, or create pollution, it all stays on Earth. The rubbish we create is still all here somewhere.

DAY AND NIGHT

Earth spins around about once in every 24 hours. This creates day and night, as one side of the Earth faces the Sun while the other is in darkness.

365 DAYS AND 940 MILLION KM

28 DAYS

24 HOURS

NORTH POLE

WINTER

SUMMER

SOUTH POLE

SEASONS

Earth is tilted slightly as it spins around. This is what causes the seasons. The tilt presents the lower part of the globe to the heat of the Sun, while the upper part is tilted away, resulting in summer and winter. As the Earth moves around the Sun, the tilt causes the opposite to also occur, so that the northern and southern hemispheres always experience opposite seasons.

HOW FAR DO WE TRAVEL IN A YEAR?

It takes one year for Earth to orbit the Sun. This is a distance of 940 million kilometres.

MOON

Poets write about the Moon and artists paint it in starry, night skies. The beautiful Moon is like a lamp in the sky, but it cannot produce any light by itself.

?

Q: Where does the light of the Moon come from?

A: The Sun! The Moon reflects sunlight back to us on Earth. The Moon is Earth's only natural satellite. Some other planets have many moons. Jupiter has 79 moons!

The Moon is about 60 to 90 million years younger than the Earth. It possibly formed when a planet the size of Mars collided with the infant Earth, resulting in a ring of shattered pieces which ended up in orbit around the Earth. This matter eventually formed the Moon.

WHAT DOES THE MOON DO FOR US?

It lights up the night sky

Some animals use moonlight as a timer in their life cycles

The Moon causes the tides in the oceans

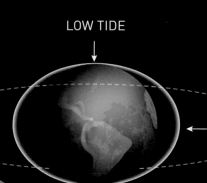

LOW TIDE

HIGH TIDE

Corals on the Great Barrier Reef rely on a number of factors, including moonlight, to spawn. This produces baby corals.

MAGNETIC EARTH

Earth has a magnetic field surrounding it. When we use a compass to find our way, we are using this magnetic field, which is what makes the compass needle point to the north.

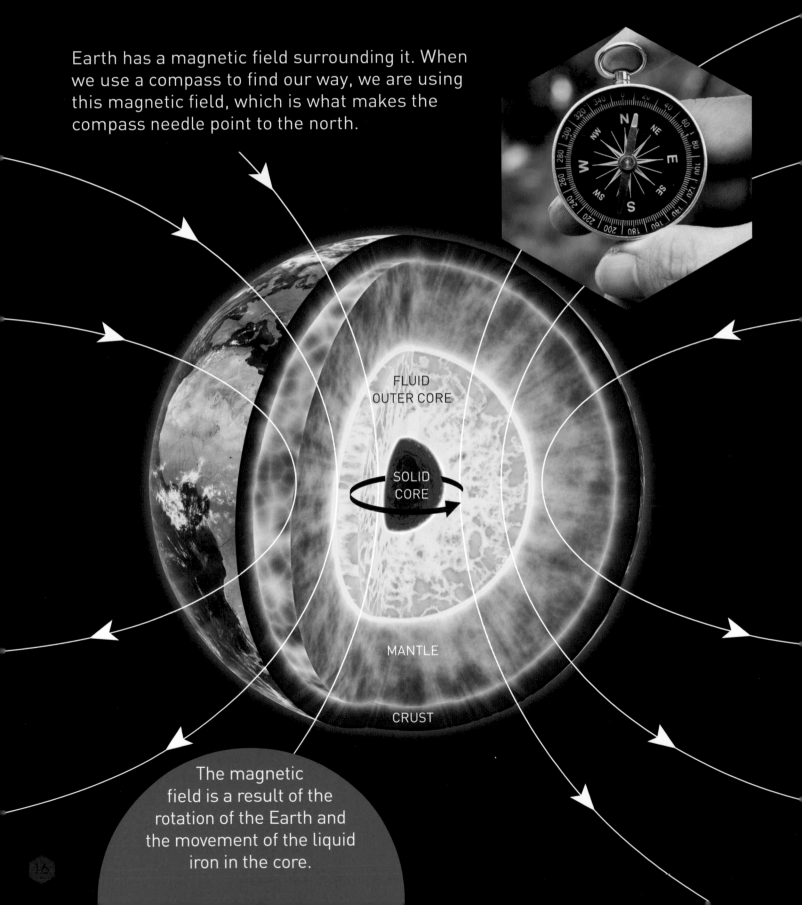

FLUID OUTER CORE

SOLID CORE

MANTLE

CRUST

The magnetic field is a result of the rotation of the Earth and the movement of the liquid iron in the core.

SOLAR WINDS

Earth's magnetic field is one of the reasons life has been able to survive on Earth. The Sun regularly sends damaging particles out into space. These solar winds interact with Earth's magnetic field, which deflects them away from us.

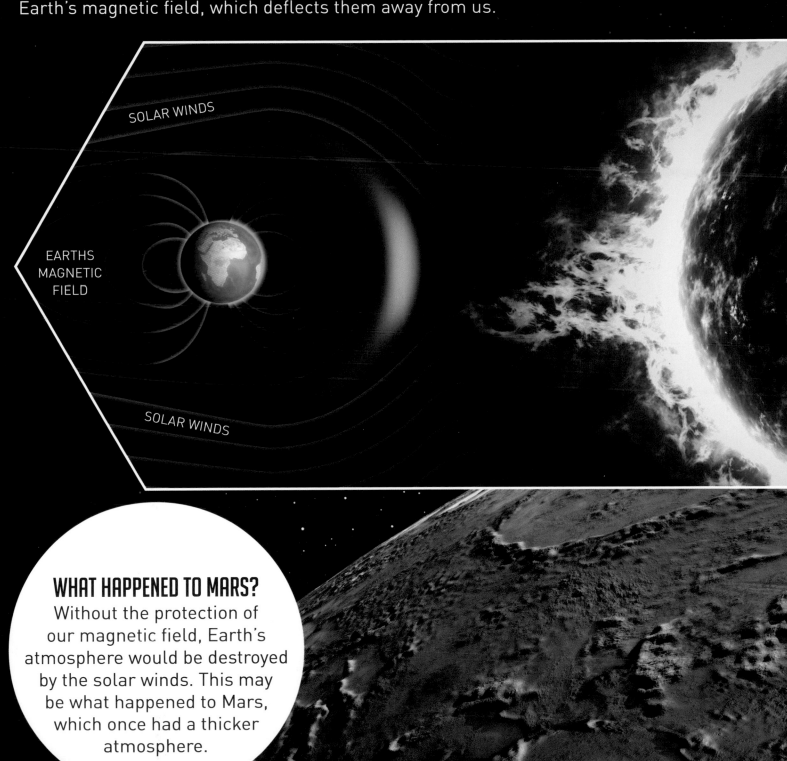

SOLAR WINDS

EARTHS MAGNETIC FIELD

SOLAR WINDS

WHAT HAPPENED TO MARS?

Without the protection of our magnetic field, Earth's atmosphere would be destroyed by the solar winds. This may be what happened to Mars, which once had a thicker atmosphere.

VOLCANOES

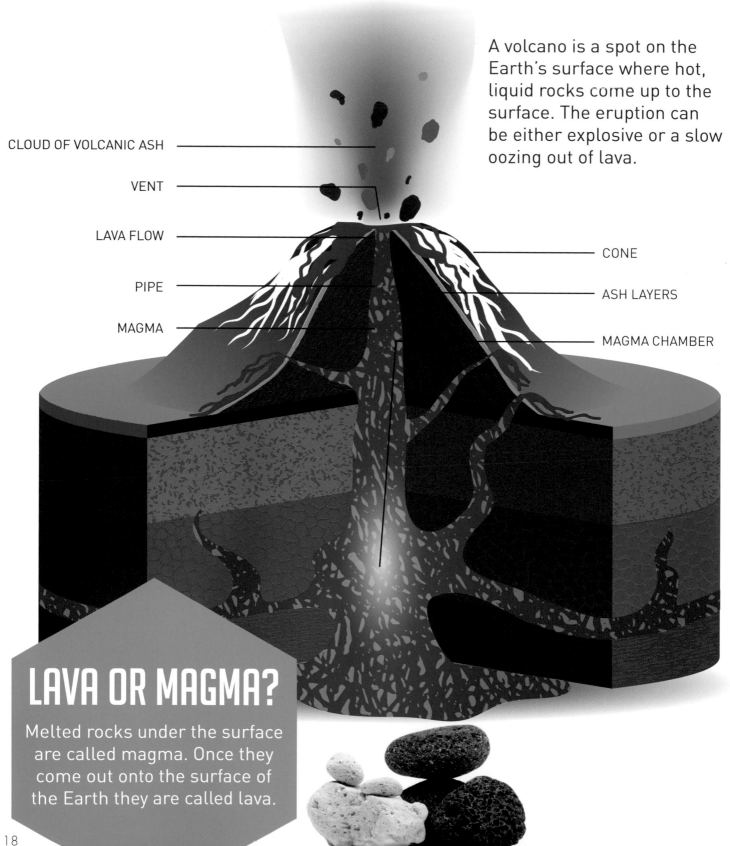

A volcano is a spot on the Earth's surface where hot, liquid rocks come up to the surface. The eruption can be either explosive or a slow oozing out of lava.

CLOUD OF VOLCANIC ASH

VENT

LAVA FLOW

PIPE

MAGMA

CONE

ASH LAYERS

MAGMA CHAMBER

LAVA OR MAGMA?

Melted rocks under the surface are called magma. Once they come out onto the surface of the Earth they are called lava.

MOUNTAIN BUILDING

Mountains form in a number of ways:

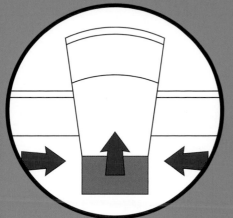

Land can be forced upwards by volcanic activity underneath it

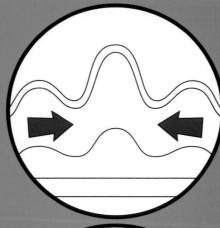

The Himalayan mountains are still being created as two land masses collide with each other and push up the rocks at the junction between them

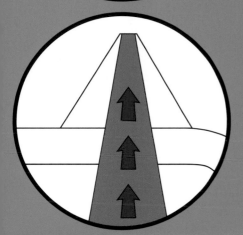

A volcano can create a large mountain in a relatively short time

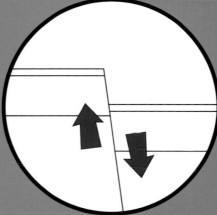

Huge blocks of rocks can break and slip down, creating a mountain with a steep side

MID-ATLANTIC RIDGE

The Mid-Atlantic Ridge extends for 16,000 kilometres under the Atlantic Ocean. Along its length there are many volcanic mountains. They form the longest mountain range in the world.

The land masses are being pulled apart along the Mid-Atlantic Ridge. As this happens, magma from the mantle below pushes up to fill the space created. This magma forms the ridge shape as well as large mountains beneath the ocean. The tops of the tallest mountains are now islands. The ridge passes right through the middle of Iceland.

EARTHQUAKES

EARTHQUAKES HAPPEN WHEN ROCKS IN THE CRUST OF THE EARTH SPLIT APART OR SLIDE PAST EACH OTHER.

SEISMIC WAVES

The energy of an earthquake spreads from where it happens outwards in seismic waves. Scientists study earthquakes by reading these waves with a seismograph.

FOCUS

The place where the actual crack or slide happens is called the focus of the earthquake.

EPICENTRE

The place on the surface directly above the focus is called the epicentre of the earthquake.

Most earthquakes happen along the edges where the continental plates meet. If these regions are in inhabited areas, there can be loss of life and property. In coastal areas, a tsunami generated by an earthquake under the ocean can send the ocean waters flooding far inland.

THE SAN ANDREAS FAULT

The San Andreas Fault line is where two of the Earth's land masses meet. It is a region of frequent earthquake activity affecting a highly populated part of the USA, including the city of San Francisco.

DEEP BENEATH OUR FEET

Have you ever wondered what's down beneath your feet? Under its surface of land and oceans, Earth has many layers.

HOW DO WE KNOW WHAT'S INSIDE THE EARTH?

Scientists have tried drilling down to find out what is inside the Earth. So far, they have never been able to drill beyond the crust, which is the Earth's hard, outer layer.

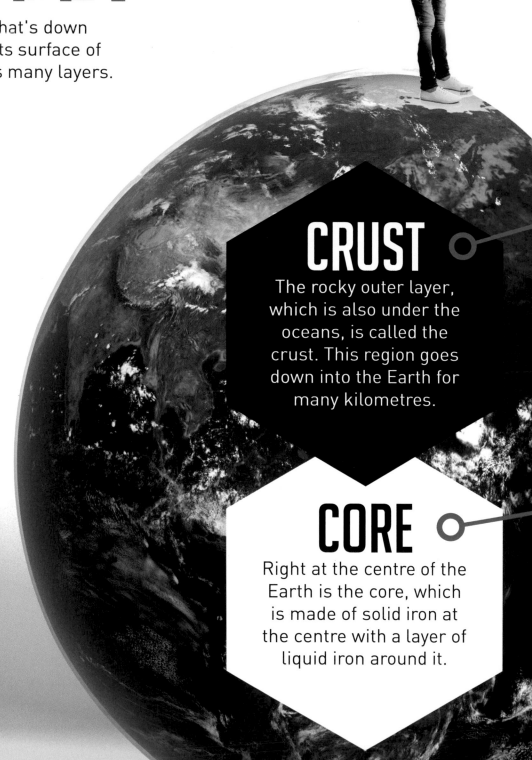

CRUST

The rocky outer layer, which is also under the oceans, is called the crust. This region goes down into the Earth for many kilometres.

CORE

Right at the centre of the Earth is the core, which is made of solid iron at the centre with a layer of liquid iron around it.

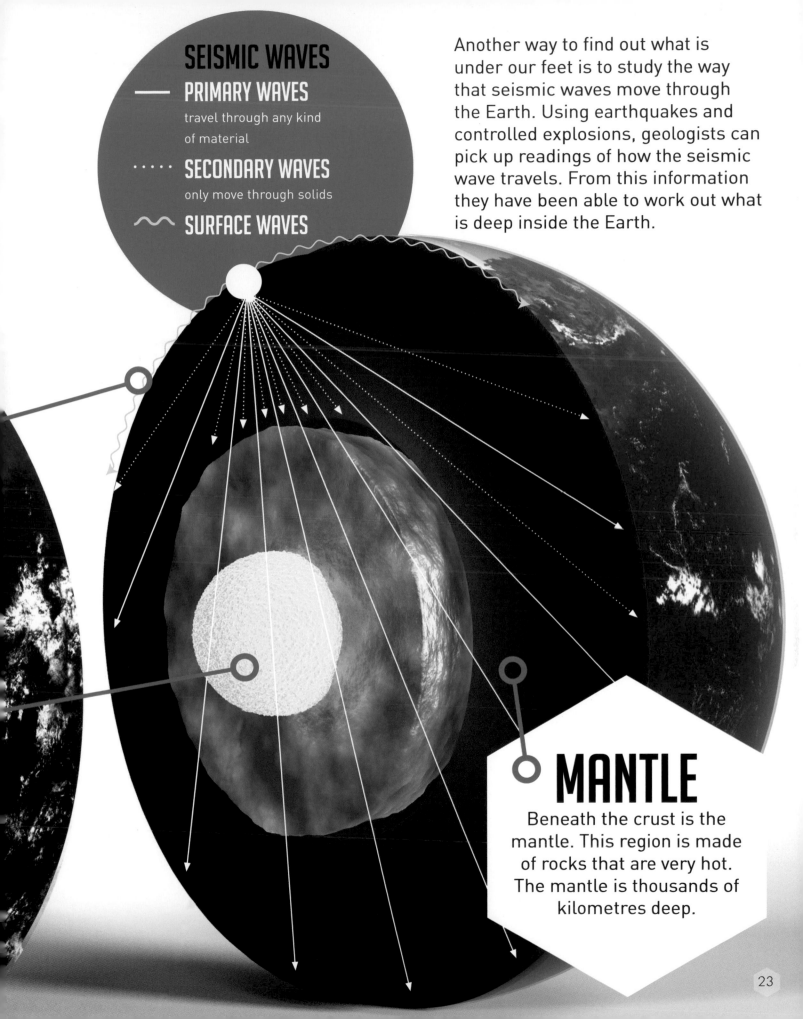

SEISMIC WAVES

—— **PRIMARY WAVES**
travel through any kind
of material

····· **SECONDARY WAVES**
only move through solids

〰 **SURFACE WAVES**

Another way to find out what is under our feet is to study the way that seismic waves move through the Earth. Using earthquakes and controlled explosions, geologists can pick up readings of how the seismic wave travels. From this information they have been able to work out what is deep inside the Earth.

MANTLE

Beneath the crust is the mantle. This region is made of rocks that are very hot. The mantle is thousands of kilometres deep.

ROCKS

Rocks form the land on Earth and the ocean floors, and they are important as building materials, sources of minerals and for their beauty in landscapes.

TYPES OF ROCKS

SEDIMENTARY ROCKS

Sedimentary rocks form when sand, other particles and the remains of living things fall to the bottom of lakes, streams and oceans, or into a depression in the land. Over millions of years, the particles compact as more matter falls on top of them. The result is sedimentary rocks.

LIMESTONE

Limestone is a sedimentary rock that forms on ocean floors when the bodies of tiny, dead organisms fall to the bottom. In Britain, the White Cliffs of Dover are made of limestone that was once deep under the ocean. The Nullarbor Plain in Australia is another area of limestone that is now dry land.

IGNEOUS ROCKS

Igneous rocks form in two ways

Solidified lava

Rocks that have formed in the heat underground. An example is granite.

Builders use marble for kitchen bench tops, and artists use it to create sculptures.

METAMORPHIC ROCKS

When a sedimentary or igneous rock experiences intense pressure or heat underground, it may turn into something different - a metamorphic rock.

MARBLE

Limestone is a sedimentary rock. If it experiences extreme heat and pressure under the ground, it turns into marble, which is a metamorphic rock.

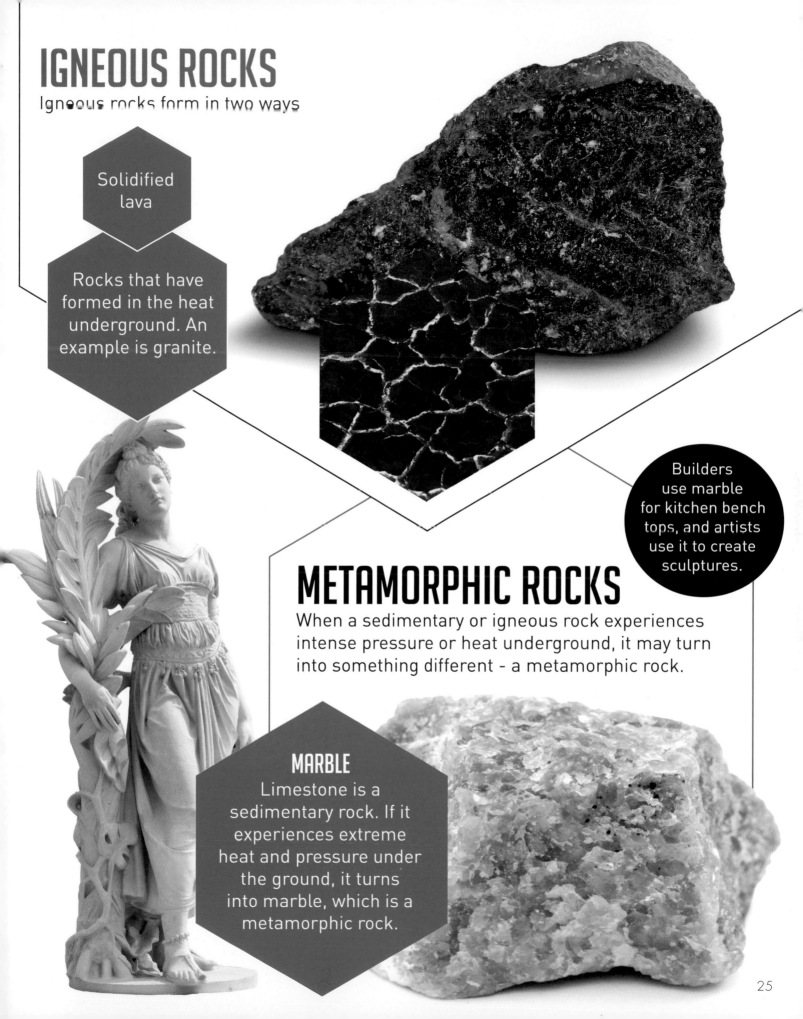

SOIL

Look at some soil under a microscope and you will see that it is has a lot of tiny particles in it. Soil is composed of many different substances all mixed together.

HUMUS

When plants and animals die, their bodies break down and contribute to humus in the soil. Plants absorb chemicals from this humus to grow.

WEATHERED ROCKS

Weathering of rocks by wind, rain, heat and cold results in the tiny particles in the rocks separating. These contribute to soil.

THE 4 LAYERS IN SOILS

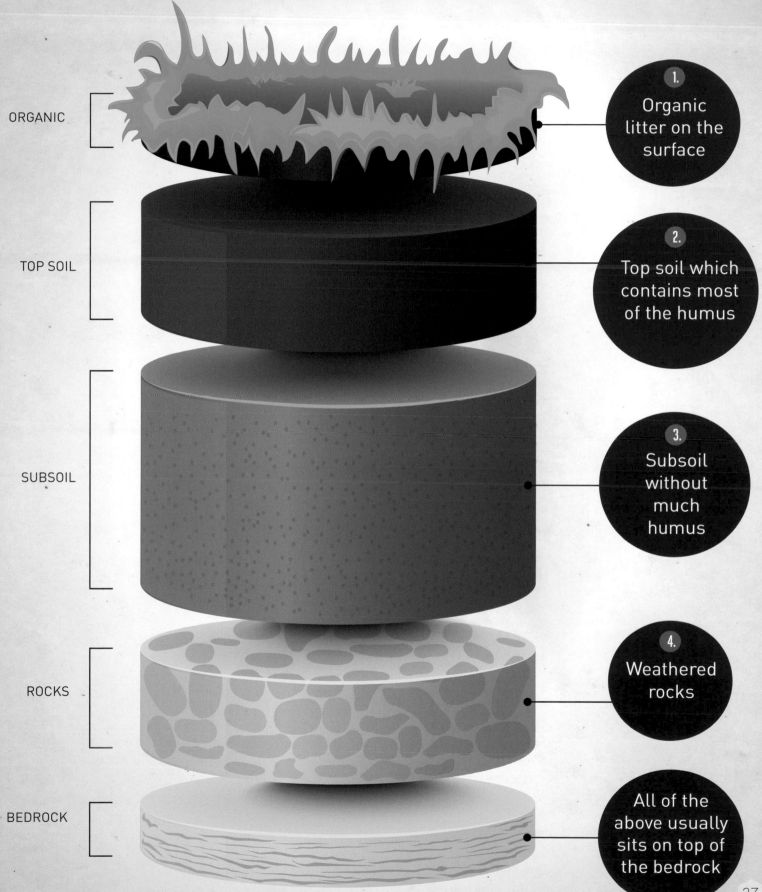

ORGANIC

TOP SOIL

SUBSOIL

ROCKS

BEDROCK

1.
Organic litter on the surface

2.
Top soil which contains most of the humus

3.
Subsoil without much humus

4.
Weathered rocks

All of the above usually sits on top of the bedrock

RESOURCES IN CYCLES

Unless there is some major event, such as an earthquake or a big storm, we expect a rock to be in the same place it was yesterday. We also expect to come home to a building that looks the same as it did when we left it earlier.

Although our surroundings on Earth seem to be much the same from day to day, everything around us is in a state of constant change. Water, carbon and even the rocks all have cycles of existence.

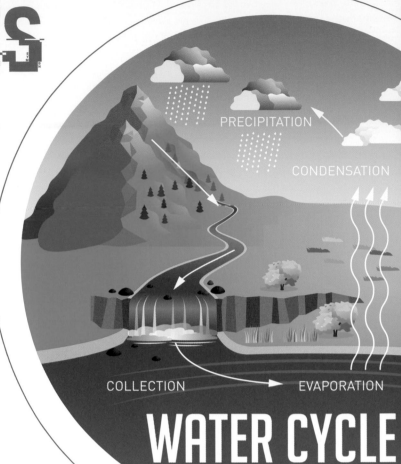

WATER CYCLE

PRECIPITATION

CONDENSATION

COLLECTION

EVAPORATION

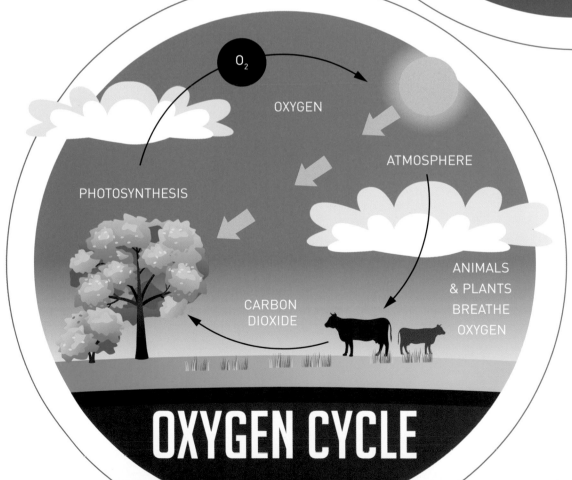

O$_2$

OXYGEN

ATMOSPHERE

PHOTOSYNTHESIS

ANIMALS & PLANTS BREATHE OXYGEN

CARBON DIOXIDE

OXYGEN CYCLE

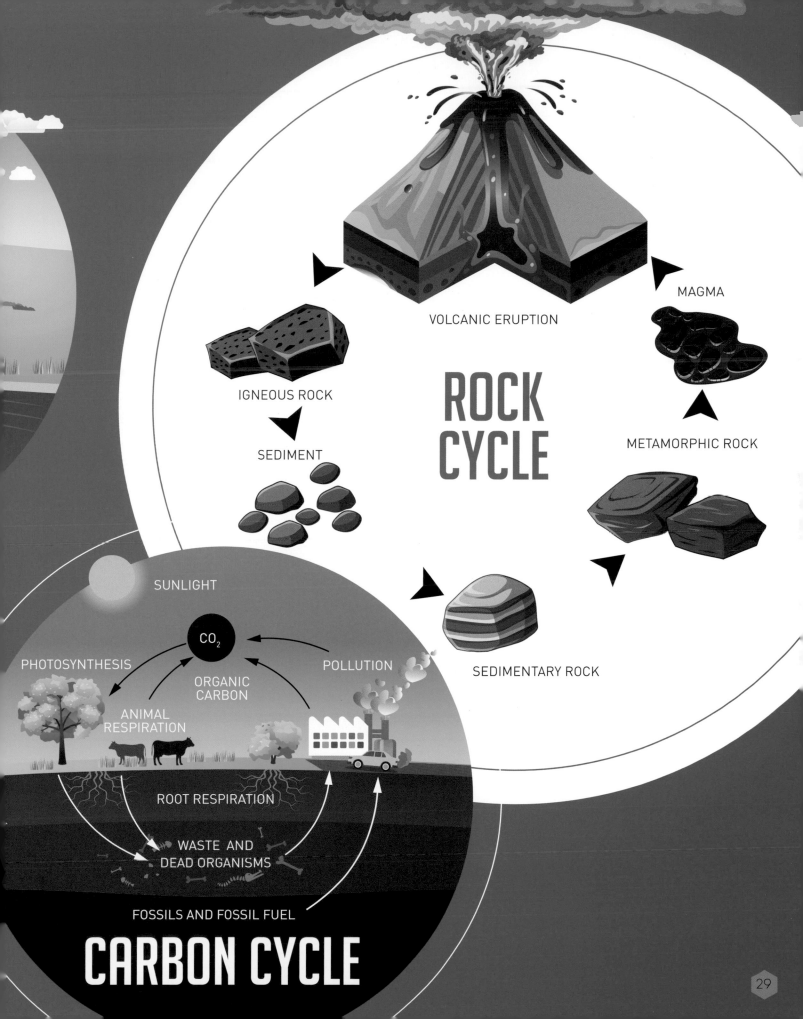

ROCK CYCLE

VOLCANIC ERUPTION

MAGMA

IGNEOUS ROCK

METAMORPHIC ROCK

SEDIMENT

SEDIMENTARY ROCK

CARBON CYCLE

SUNLIGHT

PHOTOSYNTHESIS

CO_2

ORGANIC CARBON

POLLUTION

ANIMAL RESPIRATION

ROOT RESPIRATION

WASTE AND DEAD ORGANISMS

FOSSILS AND FOSSIL FUEL

EROSION

Weathering and erosion contribute to changes in the Earth's surface features. Weathering breaks down rocks and erosion moves the products away to be deposited elsewhere.

There are many causes of weathering and erosion

DEATH OF PLANTS HOLDING SOIL IN PLACE

HEAT AND COLD CAN CAUSE ROCKS TO CRACK

ICE

HUMAN ACTIVITY

RAIN

ACIDIC RAIN CAN BREAK DOWN ROCKS CHEMICALLY

RIVERS

WIND

WAVES

GROWTH OF PLANT ROOTS THAT CRACK ROCKS APART

WORDS ABOUT OUR EARTH

bedrock rock layer underneath soil

core central part of the Earth

crust outer, hard layer of the Earth

epicentre (earthquake) place on the surface directly above the focus of an earthquake

focus (earthquake) place underground which is the source of an earthquake

fossil remains of a plant or animal found in rocks

fragile easy to destroy

fresh water water without salt in it

lava molten rock that comes to the surface of Earth

magma molten rock under the surface of Earth

magnetic field area of magnetic force

mantle part of the Earth underneath the outer crust

ooze move very slowly

ozone molecule made of three oxygen atoms

radiation energy which travels as rays or waves

satellite something orbiting the Earth

seismic waves waves that travel through the Earth as a result of an earthquake or explosion

solar system planets and other bodies orbiting a sun

solar wind expulsion of particles from the Sun

tectonics study of the way land masses move across the Earth

tsumami flood of ocean water over the land

ultraviolet light type of radiation that is dangerous to life

weathering process by which rocks and landscape features are broken down

INDEX